I0407631

CONTENTS

PREFACE

Welcome to " Hospitality in the Age of AI: Innovations and Insights for Industry Leaders." In today's rapidly evolving world, the hospitality industry stands on the threshold of a revolution driven by Artificial Intelligence (AI) and emerging technologies. This book is your essential companion in understanding, embracing, and harnessing the power of AI to reshape the landscape of your hotel business.

For hotel owners, senior management in hospitality companies, consultants, and anyone with a keen interest in the intersection of technology and the hospitality sector, this book is designed to provide a deep and insightful exploration of AI's impact. Whether you operate a boutique hotel in Mumbai, a luxury resort in Bali, or a chain of properties across the globe, the knowledge within these pages will empower you to thrive in the age of AI.

Who is This Book For?

This book is crafted with a diverse set of readers in mind, all united by a shared interest in the transformative potential of AI in hospitality:

- **Hotel Owners:** Discover how AI can optimize operations, enhance guest experiences, and drive revenue growth in your properties.

- **Senior Management in Hospitality Companies:** Gain strategic insights into how AI can be integrated into your organization's operations, from front-of-house to back-office.

- **Hospitality Consultants:** Stay ahead of industry trends and learn how to advise your clients on adopting AI technologies to stay competitive.

- Technology Enthusiasts: Satiate your curiosity about the latest technological advancements and how they are reshaping the way we experience hospitality.

What to Expect:

Our journey through the pages of this book will take you from the fundamental concepts of AI in hospitality to practical implementation strategies. We will explore real-world case studies, delve into ethical considerations, and offer an AI adoption roadmap tailored to the unique challenges of the hospitality industry.

Each chapter is meticulously crafted to provide you with actionable insights, expert perspectives, and thought-provoking discussions. You will gain a holistic understanding of AI's potential to enhance guest satisfaction, streamline operations, boost revenue, and contribute to sustainable practices in the ever-evolving world of hospitality.

Why AI in Hospitality Matters:

The hospitality industry is undergoing a profound transformation, and AI is at the forefront of this revolution. It's not just about automating tasks; it's about reimagining guest experiences, optimizing resources, and staying competitive in a dynamic market.

As we embark on this journey together, keep in mind that AI is not a replacement for human touch; it's an augmentation that empowers your staff to deliver even more exceptional service. It's about leveraging data and technology to create memorable experiences and build a sustainable, profitable future.

Thank you for joining us on this exploration of AI in the world of hospitality. By the time you finish reading this book, you will be well-equipped to make informed decisions, lead your teams, and embrace a technological future that will set your hotels apart in a highly competitive industry.

Let's embark on this transformative journey together.

THE RISE OF AI IN HOSPITALITY: A PARADIGM SHIFT IN THE HOTEL INDUSTRY

Imagine stepping into a luxurious hotel where, even before you reach the reception desk, an AI-powered chatbot on your smartphone greets you. It knows your preferences and ensures your room is personalized to your liking. This is not a scene from a sci-fi movie, but the reality of today's hospitality industry. In this chapter, we delve into the transformative role of Artificial Intelligence (AI) in the hotel industry and how it's revolutionizing guest experiences and enhancing productivity.

Personalized Guest Experience

AI enables hotels to understand their guests like never before. Leveraging data analytics, hotels can gather information about guest preferences, past stays, and behaviours. Everything from your preferred pillow type to your favourite newspaper is catered to your taste through AI.

For instance, the Wynn Las Vegas hotel has integrated Amazon's AI-powered Alexa devices into their rooms. Guests can control room temperature, lighting, and entertainment through simple voice commands. This level of personalization not only makes guests feel valued but also fosters a deeper connection with the hotel brand.

Efficient Check-In and Check-Out

The era of waiting in long queues for check-in or check-out is fading away. AI-powered kiosks and mobile apps have streamlined these processes, allowing guests to breeze through without unnecessary delays. A prime example is Hilton's "Connected Room" concept where guests can use the Hilton Honors app to check-in, select their room, and even unlock their doors.

By simplifying administrative tasks, hotel staff can focus more on delivering exceptional customer service and creating memorable experiences for guests.

Enhanced Customer Service

AI chatbots are becoming increasingly common in the hotel industry. These digital assistants are available 24/7, promptly addressing guest inquiries and providing helpful information. They can suggest nearby attractions, recommend restaurants, or even offer multilingual support, making international travellers feel at home.

Consider Marriott's AI-powered chatbot that assists guests with their requests and inquiries. By automating routine customer interactions, hotel staff can concentrate on resolving more complex issues and providing a human touch when needed.

Predictive Maintenance

Unexpected maintenance issues often lead to guest inconvenience and increased costs for hotels. However, AI comes to the rescue with predictive maintenance solutions. Through IoT sensors and AI algorithms, hotels can monitor the condition of various equipment and predict when maintenance is required.

This proactive approach helps prevent equipment breakdowns and potential guest complaints. For instance, The Cosmopolitan Hotel in Las Vegas uses AI to monitor and predict elevator maintenance needs, ensuring smooth operations and a delightful guest experience.

Personalized Recommendations

AI continues to make an impact even after a guest checks out. By analysing guest data, hotels can provide personalized offers and promotions that entice guests to return for future stays. Sending personalized emails with exclusive discounts or tailored recommendations can significantly increase customer loyalty and drive repeat business.

Conclusion

As AI continues to advance and integrate into the hotel industry, it ushers in a new era of personalized and efficient hospitality experiences. From streamlined check-ins to AI-powered chatbots, the applications are vast and exciting. Embracing AI technology enables hotels to stay competitive, boost productivity, and ultimately provide unforgettable experiences for their guests. So, business owners and managers in the hotel industry, it's time to embrace this paradigm shift!

References

:Wynn Las Vegas Hotel's use of Amazon's Alexa. : Hilton's "Connected Room" concept. : Use of AI chatbots in the hotel industry. : Marriott's AI-powered chatbot. : Use of predictive maintenance solutions in hotels. : The Cosmopolitan Hotel's use of AI for elevator maintenance. : Use of personalized recommendations in the hospitality industry. : The impact of AI on the hotel industry.

THE SMART HOTEL OF TOMORROW: IOT AND SUSTAINABLE PRACTICES IN THE HOSPITALITY SECTOR

Welcome to the future of hospitality, where hotels are not just places to stay, but technologically advanced, eco-friendly establishments that adapt seamlessly to your needs. This chapter explores the concept of the "Smart Hotel" and how the Internet of Things (IoT) is driving this transformation.

What is a Smart Hotel?

A smart hotel leverages IoT technology to create a connected ecosystem that enhances guest comfort, reduces energy consumption, and optimizes operations. Imagine a hotel that not only meets your needs but also contributes to environmental sustainability.

Smart Room Automation

In a smart hotel, your room is a marvel of technology. Sensors detect your presence and automatically adjust the temperature, lighting, and curtains to your preferences. Even if you forget to turn off the air conditioning before leaving for the day, your room can do it for you.

Pioneering examples of smart room automation include Hilton's "Connected Room" and Marriott's "Internet of Things Guestroom Lab". These initiatives showcase the potential of IoT in delivering unparalleled guest experiences.

Energy Efficiency and Sustainability

Hotels are significant energy consumers. However, with IoT, they can become more sustainable without compromising guest comfort. Smart energy management systems monitor energy usage in real-time and identify areas for conservation.

For instance, IoT-enabled thermostats adjust the temperature based on occupancy and weather conditions, reducing energy waste. Smart lighting systems ensure lights are turned off when rooms are vacant, contributing further to energy savings. These sustainable practices not only reduce a hotel's carbon footprint but also resonate with eco-conscious guests, fostering brand loyalty.

Optimized Staff Operations

The benefits of IoT extend beyond guest-facing features. For hotel staff, IoT-powered devices streamline operations and enhance productivity. Housekeeping staff receive real-time updates on room occupancy, allowing efficient task planning. IoT-enabled maintenance systems promptly identify and resolve issues, reducing downtime and improving overall service efficiency.

Enhanced Guest Safety and Security

Guest safety is paramount in the hospitality industry. IoT enhances security measures with smart surveillance and monitoring systems. IoT cameras equipped with facial recognition technology enhance hotel security and help identify potential risks. Moreover, in emergency situations, IoT-powered devices can track and manage guest flow, ensuring quick and organized evacuation.

Seamless Guest Experience

IoT technology enables hotels to offer a truly seamless and personalized guest experience. With data analytics, hotels can anticipate guest needs and preferences, providing tailored recommendations and offerings. Imagine receiving a notification about a special spa package tailored to your interests or being welcomed by name as you enter the hotel. This level of personalization creates a lasting impression on guests.

Challenges and Security Considerations

While the benefits of smart hotels are exciting, embracing IoT comes with challenges. Security is a critical concern as more devices become interconnected. Hotels must invest in robust cybersecurity measures to safeguard guest data and prevent potential breaches. Additionally, interoperability between different IoT devices and platforms requires careful consideration to ensure smooth operations and avoid compatibility issues.

Conclusion

The smart hotel of tomorrow is not a distant dream; it's rapidly approaching reality. The transformative power of IoT has the potential to revolutionize the hospitality industry by offering guests unmatched comfort while promoting sustainability and personalization.

UNDERSTANDING THE ROLE OF AI: FROM GUEST SERVICES TO OPERATIONAL EFFICIENCY

In this chapter, we delve deeper into the world of Artificial Intelligence (AI) and its multifaceted role in the hospitality industry. AI is not just about enhancing guest experiences; it also plays a crucial role in improving operational efficiency, enabling hotels to optimize their processes and resources.

AI-Powered Guest Services

AI is transforming how hotels interact with their guests, providing personalized and seamless experiences. AI-powered chatbots and virtual assistants have become invaluable tools in this regard. These digital concierges are available round-the-clock, promptly attending to guest queries and requests.

Imagine checking into your room and finding a chatbot on your smartphone that can recommend local attractions, book restaurant reservations, or even suggest the best spots for shopping. By handling repetitive tasks, AI chatbots free up hotel staff to focus on delivering exceptional customer service.

Predictive Analytics for Demand Forecasting

Hotels deal with fluctuating demand throughout the year. AI-powered predictive analytics can help hotels forecast demand accurately, allowing them to adjust pricing and inventory management accordingly. By analysing historical data, local events, and seasonal trends, AI algorithms can predict future demand patterns with high accuracy.

This enables hotels to optimize room rates, allocate resources efficiently, and avoid overbooking or underutilization of rooms. The result is increased revenue and reduced operational costs.

Personalized Marketing and Recommendations

AI is a powerful tool for creating personalized marketing campaigns. By analysing guest data and preferences, hotels can tailor promotional offers and packages to match individual tastes. AI-powered recommendation engines can suggest relevant services or activities to guests based on their past behaviour and interests.

For instance, if a guest has shown interest in spa services during previous stays, the hotel's AI system can send personalized offers for spa packages before their next visit. This targeted approach enhances guest engagement and loyalty.

Efficient Staffing and Task Management

AI is not just about enhancing guest experiences; it also helps optimize hotel operations. AI-powered workforce management tools can analyse historical data to predict staffing requirements based on expected demand. This ensures that hotels have the right number of staff members in each department to deliver top-notch service without overstaffing.

Moreover, AI can aid in task management by ensuring that staff members are assigned tasks efficiently and that all essential duties are completed promptly. This streamlines operations and improves overall productivity.

Energy Management and Sustainability

AI plays a crucial role in promoting sustainability and energy efficiency within hotels. Smart energy management systems powered by AI monitor energy consumption patterns and identify areas for optimization.

For instance, AI can analyse data from various sensors to regulate heating, ventilation, and air conditioning (HVAC) systems based on occupancy levels. This optimizes energy usage and reduces waste. Additionally, AI can help identify areas where energy-saving initiatives can be implemented, such as replacing traditional light bulbs with energy-efficient LED lights.

Enhanced Security and Fraud Detection

The safety and security of guests and their data are of utmost importance to hotels. AI-based security systems continuously monitor hotel premises, detecting any suspicious activities and potential threats.

Furthermore, AI algorithms can analyse transactions and guest behaviour to identify and prevent fraudulent activities such as credit card fraud or identity theft. This helps protect both the hotel and its guests from potential security breaches.

Conclusion

The role of AI extends beyond providing personalized guest services; it also significantly contributes to operational efficiency in the hospitality industry. By optimizing processes, improving resource allocation, enhancing security measures, and promoting sustainability practices, AI is truly revolutionizing the hospitality sector.

BEYOND THE FRONT DESK: AI-DRIVEN VIRTUAL ASSISTANTS AND CHATBOTS

In this chapter, we delve into the expanding role of AI-driven virtual assistants and chatbots in the hospitality industry. These digital companions are not just confined to the front desk; they are enhancing guest experiences and providing valuable support throughout a guest's stay.

24/7 Guest Support

AI-powered virtual assistants and chatbots are available round-the-clock, offering instant support to guests at any time of the day. Whether it's answering common inquiries, providing information about hotel amenities, or assisting with booking requests, these virtual assistants ensure that guests have access to helpful assistance whenever they need it.

Seamless Check-In and Check-Out

AI-driven virtual assistants simplify the check-in and check-out processes. Guests can complete these procedures via their smartphones or tablets, avoiding long queues at the front desk. Virtual assistants can also send automated check-out reminders and process payments, streamlining the departure experience and leaving guests with a positive last impression.

Personalized Recommendations and Suggestions

Virtual assistants and chatbots excel at understanding guest preferences and offering personalized recommendations. By analysing guest data and past interactions, these AI companions can suggest nearby attractions, popular restaurants, and other activities tailored to individual interests. This ability to offer relevant and timely suggestions enriches the guest experience and encourages guests to fully explore their surroundings.

Multilingual Support

For hotels with international guests, language barriers can pose challenges. AI-driven virtual assistants can bridge this gap by offering multilingual support. Guests can interact with chatbots in their preferred language, making them feel more at ease and improving overall communication and engagement.

Handling Guest Requests and Feedback

Virtual assistants are proficient in handling guest requests and feedback. Whether it's ordering room service, requesting extra amenities, or reporting a concern, chatbots can promptly assist guests and relay their requests to the appropriate hotel staff. Additionally, virtual assistants can analyse guest feedback to identify trends and areas for improvement, enabling hotels to continuously enhance their services based on real-time guest insights.

Contactless Solutions

Especially in a post-pandemic world, contactless solutions are highly valued by guests. AI-driven virtual assistants provide a contactless and hygienic way for guests to access information and services, reducing the need for physical touchpoints. This contactless approach aligns with guest expectations for safety and convenience, further enhancing the hotel's reputation as a tech-savvy and guest-centric establishment.

Future Possibilities

As AI technology continues to advance, the capabilities of virtual assistants and chatbots in the hospitality industry will expand further. Future possibilities include integrating AI with smart room systems, enabling guests to control room settings through voice commands or chat interactions. Moreover, as AI becomes more sophisticated, virtual assistants may develop even more human-like conversational abilities, offering guests a seamless and natural interaction experience.

Conclusion

AI-driven virtual assistants and chatbots are reshaping the guest experience in the hospitality industry. Beyond just answering queries, they offer personalized recommendations, streamline processes, and provide invaluable support throughout a guest's stay. As business owners and managers in the hospitality sector, embracing AI-driven virtual assistants is an opportunity to elevate guest service, improve operational efficiency, and cater to the preferences of tech-savvy travellers. With virtual assistants as reliable companions, hotels can create memorable experiences that leave a lasting impression.

AI-POWERED GUEST ENGAGEMENT: CREATING MEMORABLE EXPERIENCES THROUGH AI-DRIVEN INTERACTIONS

In this chapter, we delve into how AI technologies can be leveraged to create memorable guest experiences through AI-driven guest engagement. By integrating AI into various touchpoints of the guest journey, hotels can enhance interactions, exceed guest expectations, and foster lasting connections with their guests.

Personalized Pre-Arrival Communications

The guest experience begins even before guests arrive at the hotel. AI-powered pre-arrival communications can set the tone for a personalized and seamless stay. Through AI-driven messaging systems, hotels can send guests tailored communications, such as welcome messages, room upgrade offers, and suggestions for nearby attractions based on their preferences and past stays.

For instance, a business traveller who frequently stays at a hotel might receive a personalized message offering a complimentary upgrade to a premium room, recognizing their loyalty. On the other hand, a first-time leisure traveller might receive recommendations for popular local experiences and restaurants.

Seamless Check-In and In-Room Personalization

AI technologies can transform the check-in process into a smooth and frictionless experience. AI-powered self-check-in kiosks can expedite the check-in process, allowing guests to complete the necessary formalities quickly and without waiting in line.

Moreover, AI can enable in-room personalization, where guests find their preferred room settings, such as temperature and lighting, already adjusted based on their past preferences. Voice-activated assistants can further enhance in-room experiences, allowing guests to control room features, request services, and access information through simple voice commands.

AI-Driven Concierge Services

AI-powered concierge services offer guests personalized recommendations and assistance throughout their stay. Chatbots equipped with natural language processing capabilities can interact with guests, answering questions, providing information about hotel amenities, and suggesting nearby attractions and activities.

These AI-driven concierge services can operate 24/7, providing guests with instant support and recommendations at any time. Additionally, AI can analyse guest behaviour and preferences to offer targeted promotions and upsell opportunities, creating a win-win situation for guests and the hotel.

Personalized Dining Experiences

AI can enhance dining experiences by providing personalized recommendations and seamless ordering processes. AI-powered recommendation systems can analyse guest preferences and previous dining choices to suggest dishes and beverages that align with their tastes.

Moreover, AI-driven in-room dining interfaces can streamline the ordering process, making it convenient for guests to place orders and make special requests. AI can also assist with dietary restrictions and allergies, ensuring that guests receive dining options that suit their preferences and requirements.

AI for Activity Recommendations and Booking

AI technologies can assist guests in exploring the local area and booking activities. AI-powered systems can analyse guest profiles, previous bookings, and preferences to offer personalized suggestions for nearby attractions, tours, and experiences.

Additionally, AI-driven booking platforms can facilitate seamless reservations for activities and events, eliminating the need for guests to research and book independently. This level of convenience enhances guest satisfaction and encourages them to explore and enjoy the destination fully.

AI-Enhanced Guest Feedback and Service Recovery

AI plays a critical role in gathering guest feedback and resolving issues in real-time. AI-powered feedback systems collect and analyse guest reviews, social media mentions, and survey responses to identify trends and areas for improvement. Moreover, AI can detect guest sentiment from written feedback and social media posts, enabling hotels to proactively address potential issues and enhance service recovery efforts. By promptly resolving guest concerns, hotels can turn negative experiences into positive ones, improving guest loyalty and satisfaction.

AI-Driven Loyalty and Rewards Programs

AI technologies can revolutionize loyalty and rewards programs, making them more personalized and enticing for guests. AI-powered loyalty platforms analyse guest data to offer targeted rewards and incentives that resonate with individual preferences and stay patterns. For instance, a frequent business traveller might receive exclusive loyalty offers for weekday stays, while a leisure traveller might receive rewards for booking longer weekend stays. AI can also predict future travel patterns and offer personalized promotions to encourage repeat bookings and enhance guest retention.

Predictive Guest Services

AI-powered predictive analytics can anticipate guest needs and provide anticipatory service. By analysing guest behaviour and historical data, AI can predict preferences and proactively offer services, such as a spa treatment reservation based on a guest's previous interest in spa services. Additionally, AI can predict guest demand for certain amenities or services during peak times, allowing hotels to allocate resources more efficiently and enhance guest satisfaction.

Emotional AI and Guest Engagement

Emotional AI, also known as affective computing, enables AI systems to recognize and respond to human emotions. Implementing emotional AI in guest engagement allows hotels to create more empathetic and emotionally resonant interactions. Emotional AI can analyse facial expressions and tone of voice to gauge guest emotions during interactions. For example, if a guest expresses frustration with a service, emotional AI can detect this emotion and respond with empathy, assuring the guest that the issue will be resolved promptly.

Leveraging AI for Post-Stay Engagement

The guest experience doesn't end when guests check out. AI plays a crucial role in post-stay engagement and guest retention. AI-powered post-stay surveys gather feedback and insights from guests about their overall experience. Furthermore, AI personalizes post-stay communications, expressing gratitude for the guest's stay and offering incentives for future bookings. AI identifies potential repeat guests and sends targeted promotions to encourage their return, fostering long-term loyalty and guest relationships.

Conclusion

AI technologies offer boundless opportunities to create memorable guest experiences and drive guest engagement in the hospitality industry. By integrating AI into various touchpoints of the guest journey, hotels can deliver personalized services, streamline operations, and exceed guest expectations.

From personalized pre-arrival communications to AI-driven concierge services and dining experiences, AI enhances guest interactions at every stage of their stay. AI-driven loyalty programs foster guest loyalty while predictive guest services enhance satisfaction. Emotional AI adds empathy to guest engagement.

AI technologies also play a crucial role in gathering feedback from guests, enabling hotels to continuously improve their services based on real-time insights. Additionally, post-stay engagement supported by AI ensures that the hotel remains connected with guests even after their departure.

By embracing AI-driven guest engagement, hotels elevate their service standards while creating memorable experiences that leave lasting impressions on their guests.

SMART GUEST EXPERIENCE: PERSONALIZATION AND AI-DRIVEN RECOMMENDATIONS

Welcome to a new chapter focused on the ever-evolving concept of the "Smart Guest Experience." In this chapter, we'll explore how Artificial Intelligence (AI) is transforming the way hotels cater to their guests, providing personalized services and AI-driven recommendations that leave a lasting impression.

The Power of Personalization

In the digital age, guests expect more than just a comfortable stay; they seek personalized experiences that cater to their unique preferences. AI enables hotels to gather and analyse vast amounts of guest data, allowing them to understand individual needs and desires better. From the moment a guest books a room, AI can start building a profile based on past stays, preferences, and interactions. This information is then used to curate a personalized experience, ensuring that each guest feels valued and special.

Tailored Room Preferences

Imagine arriving at a hotel, and your room is already set up just the way you like it. From the choice of pillows and room temperature to the preferred type of tea in the minibar, AI can ensure that your room is personalized to your taste even before you step in. Marriott's "Bonvoy" loyalty program is a prime example of AI-driven personalization. By analysing guest data, the program tailors offers and services to individual preferences, creating a unique and delightful experience for each member.

AI-Driven Recommendations

AI excels at making data-driven decisions, and this applies to recommendations as well. Hotel guests are often eager to explore local attractions, restaurants, and activities. AI can analyse guest profiles, historical data, and real-time information about local events to offer personalized recommendations. For instance, if a guest has a penchant for art museums, the hotel's AI system can suggest nearby art galleries and exhibitions. By providing relevant and timely recommendations, hotels can elevate the guest experience and foster a sense of discovery.

Personalized Dining Experiences

The culinary aspect of a guest's stay can also be enhanced through personalization. AI-powered systems can track guests' dietary preferences, allergies, and past dining experiences to offer tailored restaurant suggestions and menu options. Moreover, hotels can employ AI chatbots or virtual concierges to make dining reservations based on guest preferences. This streamlined approach saves time and ensures that guests can enjoy their favourite cuisines without hassle.

Proactive Service and Anticipatory Hospitality

With AI's predictive capabilities, hotels can anticipate guest needs even before they express them. By analysing guest behaviour, past requests, and external factors, AI can proactively offer services and amenities that align with individual preferences. For example, if a hotel knows that a guest enjoys morning yoga sessions, the AI system can set a reminder for the yoga class schedule and offer to arrange a mat in the guest's room. This anticipatory hospitality leaves guests feeling cared for and creates an unforgettable experience.

Enhancing Loyalty and Repeat Business

Personalized guest experiences powered by AI not only impress guests during their stay but also create a lasting impact that extends beyond checkout. When guests feel genuinely valued, they are more likely to become loyal patrons, returning for future stays and recommending the hotel to others. Loyal guests contribute significantly to a hotel's bottom line, and AI-driven personalization is a potent tool for fostering guest loyalty and repeat business.

Conclusion

The Smart Guest Experience powered by AI is all about making guests feel special and catered to at every touchpoint of their stay. Through personalization and AI-driven recommendations, hotels can elevate guest satisfaction, enhance loyalty, and stand out in an increasingly competitive market.

AI-POWERED REVENUE MANAGEMENT: OPTIMIZING OCCUPANCY AND PRICING STRATEGIES

Welcome to the world of AI-driven revenue management in the hospitality industry. In this chapter, we'll explore how Artificial Intelligence (AI) is transforming the way hotels optimize their occupancy and pricing strategies, enabling them to maximize revenue and stay competitive in a dynamic market.

The Complexity of Revenue Management

Managing room rates and occupancy levels is a complex task for hotels. The goal is to achieve maximum revenue by selling the right room at the right price to the right customer at the right time. This requires a deep understanding of demand patterns, market dynamics, and guest behaviour. AI is the key to unlocking the full potential of revenue management, as it can process vast amounts of data quickly and make data-driven decisions that were previously challenging for humans to handle.

Demand Forecasting and Pricing Optimization

AI's predictive analytics capabilities are instrumental in forecasting demand accurately. By analysing historical booking data, local events, seasonality, and other factors, AI algorithms can predict future demand patterns with greater accuracy than traditional methods. With this foresight, hotels can adjust room rates dynamically, optimizing prices based on demand fluctuations. AI-powered pricing strategies allow hotels to maximize revenue during peak periods while still offering attractive rates during periods of lower demand.

Dynamic Pricing and Real-Time Adjustments

Dynamic pricing is a key aspect of AI-driven revenue management. Instead of fixed rates, hotels can employ dynamic pricing models that change in real-time based on factors such as demand, availability, and market conditions. For instance, if a hotel anticipates low occupancy for a particular day, AI can trigger real-time rate discounts to attract more bookings. Conversely, during periods of high demand, AI can increase rates to capitalize on higher revenue potential.

Personalized Offers and Upselling

AI can also help hotels personalize offers and upsell additional services based on individual guest preferences. By analysing guest data and booking history, hotels can identify opportunities to offer tailored packages or complementary services that align with guest interests. For example, if a guest has booked a room with a sea view, the hotel's AI system can suggest an upgrade to a suite with a private balcony, enticing the guest with a personalized offer.

Competitive Market Analysis

AI-powered revenue management goes beyond analysing internal data. It can also monitor competitor pricing and market trends to provide insights on how to position a hotel in the market effectively. By understanding competitors' pricing strategies and demand patterns, hotels can adjust their own pricing and marketing strategies to remain competitive and capture market share.

Balancing Occupancy and Profitability

One of the primary goals of AI-driven revenue management is to strike the right balance between maximizing occupancy and maintaining profitability. While high occupancy is desirable, it shouldn't come at the expense of lowering rates excessively, impacting revenue. AI algorithms consider both occupancy goals and revenue targets to achieve an optimal balance, ensuring that hotels can maintain profitability even during periods of high demand.

Conclusion

AI-powered revenue management is a game-changer for the hospitality industry. By leveraging AI's predictive capabilities, hotels can optimize their occupancy and pricing strategies, increase revenue, and make data-driven decisions with confidence. As business owners and managers in the hospitality sector, embracing AI-driven revenue management can help your hotel stay ahead of the competition and adapt to ever-changing market conditions. With AI as your ally, you can unlock new levels of revenue optimization and create a more prosperous future.

SUSTAINABILITY SOLUTIONS: GREEN INITIATIVES AND AI'S IMPACT ON HOTELS

Welcome to a chapter focused on sustainability in the hospitality industry. In recent years, there has been a growing awareness of the need for eco-friendly practices in hotels. In this chapter, we'll explore how Artificial Intelligence (AI) is playing a pivotal role in driving green initiatives and helping hotels become more sustainable.

The Call for Sustainable Practices

As environmental concerns escalate, guests increasingly prefer eco-conscious hotels that actively contribute to environmental preservation. Embracing sustainability not only benefits the planet but also enhances a hotel's reputation and appeals to eco-conscious travellers.

AI-Driven Energy Management

AI is instrumental in optimizing energy consumption, one of the most significant environmental challenges hotels face. AI-powered energy management systems use sensors and data analytics to monitor energy usage throughout the hotel. By analysing occupancy levels and guest behaviour, AI can adjust heating, cooling, and lighting systems in real-time, ensuring energy is utilized efficiently without compromising guest comfort. Additionally, AI can identify energy-saving opportunities and recommend sustainable solutions to reduce the hotel's carbon footprint.

Waste Reduction and Recycling

AI can also contribute to waste reduction efforts. Smart waste management systems, integrated with AI, can monitor waste production and disposal patterns. AI algorithms analyse this data to identify opportunities for waste reduction and recycling. For instance, AI can suggest ways to reduce single-use plastics, encourage proper recycling practices, and optimize waste collection routes to minimize environmental impact.

Water Conservation Strategies

Water conservation is another vital aspect of sustainability for hotels. AI-driven smart water management systems monitor water usage patterns throughout the property. By detecting leaks or excessive water usage in real-time, AI helps hotels identify areas where water conservation efforts can be improved. Implementing water-saving technologies, such as low-flow faucets and showerheads, can also be guided by AI insights.

Green Procurement and Supply Chain Optimization

AI can assist hotels in adopting green procurement practices. By analysing supplier data and sustainability certifications, AI algorithms can recommend eco-friendly suppliers and products that align with a hotel's sustainability goals. Furthermore, AI can optimize supply chain logistics, reducing transportation-related emissions and minimizing the hotel's overall environmental impact.

Data-Driven Sustainability Metrics

AI empowers hotels to track and measure their sustainability performance with data-driven metrics. By collecting and analysing sustainability-related data, hotels can monitor their progress towards environmental goals and make informed decisions on further improvements. Transparently sharing these sustainability metrics with guests also demonstrates a commitment to environmental responsibility and fosters trust in the hotel's green initiatives.

Conclusion

AI's impact on sustainability in the hospitality industry is profound. By leveraging AI-driven solutions, hotels can significantly reduce their environmental footprint, enhance operational efficiency, and meet the expectations of eco-conscious guests. As business owners and managers in the hospitality sector, embracing AI for sustainability solutions not only benefits the environment but also drives positive guest perceptions and loyalty. AI and green initiatives together form a winning combination that sets hotels on the path to a more sustainable future.

AI-ENHANCED SAFETY AND SECURITY: ENSURING GUEST WELL-BEING

In this chapter, we'll explore how Artificial Intelligence (AI) is revolutionizing safety and security in the hospitality industry. By leveraging advanced AI technologies, hotels can create a secure and reassuring environment for their guests, prioritizing their well-being at every step.

Smart Surveillance and Monitoring

AI-powered surveillance systems equipped with sophisticated cameras and facial recognition capabilities play a pivotal role in enhancing hotel security. These systems can monitor key areas, such as entrances, lobbies, and parking lots, in real-time, alerting security personnel of any suspicious activity. Additionally, AI can analyse guest behaviour to detect anomalies, such as individuals loitering in restricted areas or unusual patterns of movement, allowing security teams to respond promptly to potential security threats.

Contactless Check-In and Access Control

AI has been instrumental in driving contactless solutions, especially during the COVID-19 pandemic. Contactless check-in and access control systems leverage AI-powered facial recognition or mobile technology to enable seamless and secure guest entry without the need for physical touchpoints. Not only does this streamline the check-in process, but it also minimizes the risk of transmission of viruses and enhances guest confidence in the hotel's commitment to their safety.

Predictive Maintenance for Safety

AI's predictive capabilities extend beyond security. It can also be used for predictive maintenance to ensure guest safety. By analysing data from various sensors and equipment, AI can identify potential maintenance issues before they escalate into safety hazards. For instance, AI can detect abnormalities in fire alarm systems or elevator operations, allowing hotels to address any safety concerns promptly and proactively.

Emergency Response and Evacuation Planning

In case of emergencies, AI can assist in emergency response and evacuation planning. AI-driven systems can track guest movement within the hotel, allowing security teams to quickly identify the location of guests in case of an evacuation. Moreover, AI can analyse various factors, such as occupancy levels and building layout, to optimize evacuation routes and ensure a safe and efficient evacuation process.

Protecting Guest Data with AI

Data security is paramount in the hospitality industry, as hotels handle vast amounts of sensitive guest information. AI can bolster data security measures by continuously monitoring network activity for any unusual behaviour indicative of a cyberattack. Additionally, AI can identify potential vulnerabilities in the hotel's IT infrastructure and recommend security upgrades to safeguard guest data from data breaches and other cyber threats.

Guest Safety in Shared Spaces

Hotels often have shared spaces such as swimming pools, gyms, and restaurants where guest safety must be a top priority. AI can help enforce safety protocols, such as capacity limits and social distancing measures, in these areas. AI-powered cameras and sensors can monitor crowd density and alert staff when capacity limits are approaching, ensuring that guests can safely enjoy these amenities.

Conclusion

AI-enhanced safety and security solutions are transforming the hospitality industry by prioritizing guest well-being and providing a secure environment. From smart surveillance to contactless access control, AI technologies contribute to a comprehensive safety strategy that inspires confidence among guests. As business owners and managers in the hospitality sector, adopting AI-driven safety and security measures not only ensures guest satisfaction and loyalty but also upholds the hotel's reputation as a safe haven for travellers. With AI as a trusted ally, hotels can continually enhance their safety protocols and deliver peace of mind to their valued guests.

STREAMLINING OPERATIONS: AI FOR EFFICIENT HOTEL MANAGEMENT

In this chapter, we'll explore how Artificial Intelligence (AI) is revolutionizing hotel management and streamlining various operational aspects. From optimizing staff schedules to managing inventory and improving overall efficiency, AI is a game-changer for hotel operations.

Optimizing Staff Scheduling and Workforce Management

AI-powered workforce management tools take the guesswork out of staff scheduling. By analysing historical data, guest booking patterns, and upcoming events, AI algorithms can predict staffing needs accurately. This ensures that hotels have the right number of staff members in each department at the right times, leading to improved service levels, reduced labour costs, and increased staff satisfaction.

Efficient Inventory Management

AI plays a crucial role in optimizing inventory management in hotels. Whether it's managing supplies for the restaurant, minibars in guest rooms, or amenities for the spa, AI can analyse data to predict demand and track inventory levels in real-time. Automated inventory systems with AI algorithms can alert hotel staff when supplies are running low, preventing stockouts and ensuring that guests' needs are always met.

Streamlining Housekeeping Operations

Housekeeping is a critical part of hotel operations, and AI can enhance its efficiency. By analysing guest check-out times and room occupancy data, AI can optimize the cleaning schedule, ensuring that rooms are prepared promptly for new arrivals. Additionally, AI-powered robotic vacuums and cleaning machines can handle routine tasks, freeing up housekeeping staff to focus on more specialized services and guest requests.

Automated Guest Feedback Analysis

AI-driven sentiment analysis tools are invaluable for hotel management. They can analyse guest feedback from various sources, such as online reviews and surveys, to identify trends and sentiment. By gaining insights into guest preferences and areas for improvement, hotel management can make data-driven decisions to enhance the guest experience and address any issues promptly.

Predictive Maintenance for Equipment

AI's predictive maintenance capabilities extend to hotel equipment as well. By monitoring the performance of various systems, such as HVAC, elevators, and kitchen appliances, AI can predict potential maintenance issues before they lead to costly breakdowns. With timely maintenance, hotels can reduce downtime, prevent guest inconveniences, and extend the lifespan of expensive equipment.

Efficient Energy Consumption

AI-powered energy management systems not only contribute to sustainability but also help control operational costs. By analysing energy consumption patterns, AI can optimize the usage of lighting, heating, and cooling systems to reduce energy waste. Intelligent control of energy usage leads to cost savings and supports a hotel's commitment to environmental responsibility.

Conclusion

AI's impact on hotel management is far-reaching, transforming various operational aspects and leading to enhanced efficiency and cost-effectiveness. By leveraging AI's predictive capabilities, hotels can optimize staff scheduling, inventory management, and maintenance practices while providing a seamless and delightful experience for their guests. As business owners and managers in the hospitality industry, embracing AI for efficient hotel management is a strategic move that allows you to stay ahead of the competition while delivering exceptional service and managing operational costs effectively.

DATA ANALYTICS AND INSIGHTS: LEVERAGING AI FOR INFORMED DECISION-MAKING

In this chapter, we'll explore the power of data analytics and how Artificial Intelligence (AI) can transform raw data into actionable insights, enabling hotels to make informed decisions that drive success and guest satisfaction.

The Data Revolution in Hospitality

Hotels accumulate vast amounts of data every day, including guest preferences, booking patterns, operational metrics, and more. However, raw data alone does not provide meaningful value; it's the analysis and interpretation of this data that can unlock its true potential. AI-driven data analytics tools have the ability to process and analyse large datasets rapidly, uncovering valuable patterns, trends, and correlations that can inform strategic decision-making.

Personalizing the Guest Experience

One of the key applications of data analytics is personalization. By analysing guest data, hotels can gain insights into individual preferences, stay histories, and spending behaviour. Armed with this information, hotels can offer personalized recommendations, promotions, and special offers tailored to each guest's interests. Personalization enhances guest satisfaction and fosters a stronger connection between guests and the hotel brand.

Demand Forecasting and Revenue Optimization

Data analytics, powered by AI algorithms, is instrumental in demand forecasting. By analysing historical data and external factors such as local events and weather patterns, hotels can predict future demand with greater accuracy. Accurate demand forecasts enable hotels to optimize pricing strategies, ensuring that room rates are adjusted dynamically to match demand fluctuations. This approach maximizes revenue and ensures that hotels achieve optimal occupancy levels.

Operational Efficiency and Cost Reduction

Data analytics can uncover inefficiencies and areas for cost reduction within hotel operations. By analysing data related to staff performance, inventory management, and energy consumption, hotels can identify opportunities to streamline operations and minimize expenses. For instance, data analytics can reveal patterns of energy waste, prompting hotels to implement energy-saving measures that reduce utility costs while promoting sustainability.

Reputation Management and Guest Feedback

Online reviews and guest feedback are valuable sources of information for hotels. AI-driven sentiment analysis tools can analyse guest sentiments expressed in reviews and social media comments. By understanding guest sentiment, hotels can address concerns promptly and improve services based on valuable feedback. Managing online reputation is vital in the digital age, and data analytics helps hotels stay on top of guest perceptions and respond proactively to maintain a positive image.

Benchmarking and Competitive Analysis

Data analytics also enables hotels to benchmark their performance against competitors. By analysing data related to competitor pricing, guest reviews, and market trends, hotels can gain insights into their competitive position. This information empowers hotels to refine their strategies, identify areas for improvement, and capitalize on market opportunities to stay ahead of the competition.

Conclusion

Data analytics empowered by AI is a transformative force in the hospitality industry. By extracting insights from data, hotels can optimize guest experiences, revenue management, and operational efficiency. As business owners and managers in the hospitality sector, leveraging data analytics and AI-driven insights is critical for staying competitive and making informed decisions that drive success. The ability to harness data effectively enables hotels to continuously enhance guest satisfaction, drive revenue growth, and achieve sustainable success in a dynamic and ever-evolving market.

AI INTEGRATION CHALLENGES: OVERCOMING OBSTACLES TO IMPLEMENTATION

In this chapter, we'll discuss the challenges that hotels may encounter when implementing AI solutions and explore strategies to overcome these obstacles successfully.

Data Quality and Accessibility

One of the primary challenges in AI implementation is ensuring that the data used for analysis is of high quality and accessible. Hotels collect vast amounts of data, but it may be scattered across different systems or stored in varying formats. To address this, hotels must invest in data management systems that consolidate and organize data from various sources. Additionally, ensuring data accuracy and consistency is crucial to obtain reliable insights from AI algorithms.

Costs and ROI Concerns

AI implementation may involve significant upfront costs, leading to concerns about return on investment (ROI). Hotels may be hesitant to invest in AI technologies without a clear understanding of their potential benefits and cost savings. To address this, hotels should conduct a thorough cost-benefit analysis and consider long-term advantages. AI's ability to enhance operational efficiency, personalize guest experiences, and drive revenue growth can significantly outweigh initial investments.

Staff Training and Adoption

AI technologies often require specialized skills for implementation and maintenance. Training existing staff or hiring new personnel with AI expertise may be necessary, which can be a challenge in itself. To overcome this obstacle, hotels should invest in staff training programs and foster a culture of technological adaptation. Involving employees in the AI integration process and showcasing the benefits can foster enthusiasm and increase staff adoption.

Data Privacy and Security

With the use of AI comes concerns about data privacy and security. Hotels deal with sensitive guest information, and the improper handling of data can lead to breaches and legal consequences. To address data privacy concerns, hotels must implement robust cybersecurity measures, comply with relevant regulations (e.g., GDPR), and establish strict data access controls. Transparency in data usage and communication with guests about data handling can also build trust.

Interoperability and Integration

Hotels often use multiple software systems for different operations. Ensuring that AI solutions can integrate seamlessly with existing systems is essential for efficient implementation. To tackle interoperability challenges, hotels should choose AI solutions that offer open APIs (Application Programming Interfaces) for easy integration. Collaborating with tech vendors who specialize in hospitality AI can also facilitate smooth integration.

Overcoming Resistance to Change

Introducing AI technologies may be met with resistance from staff or even guests who may prefer traditional processes. To overcome resistance, clear communication about the benefits of AI and its role in enhancing guest experiences and staff efficiency is vital. Demonstrating successful AI use cases and showing tangible improvements can convince stakeholders of AI's value.

Conclusion

AI integration in the hospitality industry brings great promise, but it also comes with its share of challenges. By addressing data quality, costs, staff training, data privacy, interoperability, and resistance to change, hotels can successfully implement AI solutions that drive business success and elevate the guest experience. As business owners and managers in the hospitality sector, being proactive in addressing these challenges ensures a smoother AI adoption process and positions hotels for sustainable growth in a tech-driven world.

AI ETHICS AND GUEST PRIVACY: STRIKING THE RIGHT BALANCE

In this chapter, we'll explore the ethical considerations surrounding AI implementation in the hospitality industry and how hotels can ensure guest privacy while harnessing the benefits of AI technologies.

The Ethical Dilemma: Balancing Innovation and Privacy

As hotels integrate AI technologies into their operations, they must grapple with the ethical dilemma of balancing innovation and guest privacy. While AI offers numerous advantages, it also raises concerns about data collection, surveillance, and potential misuse of guest information. Hotels must prioritize guest privacy and establish ethical guidelines for the responsible use of AI to build trust and protect guest data.

Informed Consent and Transparent Communication

Obtaining informed consent from guests is paramount when collecting and using their personal data for AI-driven services. Hotels should clearly communicate the purpose, scope, and potential risks associated with data collection and use. Transparent communication fosters trust between hotels and guests, ensuring that guests are aware of how their data will be used and empowering them to make informed decisions about their privacy.

Anonymization and Data Minimization

To enhance guest privacy, hotels should adopt practices such as anonymization and data minimization. Anonymizing data removes personally identifiable information, making it less susceptible to privacy breaches. Data minimization involves collecting only the necessary data to achieve specific AI-driven objectives, reducing the risk of exposing sensitive information.

Securing Guest Data

Hotels must prioritize data security to protect guest information from unauthorized access or data breaches. Implementing robust cybersecurity measures, encryption, and access controls are essential steps to safeguard guest data. Partnering with reputable tech vendors and service providers who prioritize data security can also enhance guest privacy.

Compliance with Data Protection Regulations

Hotels must adhere to relevant data protection regulations, such as the General Data Protection Regulation (GDPR) in the European Union. Compliance with these regulations ensures that guest data is handled responsibly and that guests have control over their personal information. Staying up-to-date with evolving data protection laws and ensuring that AI practices align with these regulations is critical for maintaining guest trust.

Human Oversight and Intervention

While AI technologies automate various processes, human oversight and intervention are essential to ensure ethical decision-making. Human intervention can prevent AI from making biased or unfair judgments, especially in areas such as guest profiling and recommendation systems. Hotels should strike a balance between AI-driven automation and the human touch to preserve the personalized and empathetic nature of hospitality.

Conclusion

AI technologies offer tremendous potential to transform the hospitality industry and elevate guest experiences. However, hotels must approach AI implementation with a strong commitment to ethics and guest privacy. By obtaining informed consent, ensuring transparent communication, anonymizing data, securing guest information, and complying with data protection regulations, hotels can strike the right balance between innovation and privacy. Upholding ethical AI practices not only safeguards guest privacy but also reinforces the hotel's reputation as a trustworthy and responsible establishment that values its guests' well-being.

THE HUMAN ELEMENT: AI'S COLLABORATION WITH HOTEL STAFF

In this chapter, we'll explore how AI technologies can collaborate with hotel staff, enhancing their capabilities and augmenting their roles to provide even better guest experiences.

Empowering Staff with AI Insights

AI-powered analytics can provide valuable insights to hotel staff, enabling them to make data-driven decisions and offer personalized guest experiences. By analysing guest preferences and behaviour, AI can help staff anticipate guest needs and tailor their interactions accordingly. For instance, knowing a guest's favourite amenities or dining preferences allows staff to provide personalized recommendations and surprises, creating memorable moments for guests.

Efficient Customer Support with Chatbots

AI-driven chatbots are valuable tools for hotel staff, streamlining customer support and reducing response times. Instead of handling routine inquiries, staff can focus on more complex guest requests that require a human touch. Chatbots can handle reservation inquiries, provide information about hotel amenities, and offer assistance with common guest questions, freeing up staff to deliver more personalized services.

Enhancing Language Capabilities

For hotels catering to an international clientele, language barriers can be a challenge. AI-powered language translation tools can help overcome these obstacles by enabling staff to communicate effectively with guests who speak different languages. Language translation AI tools can facilitate smooth interactions, ensuring that guests feel comfortable and well-cared for, regardless of their native language.

AI-Assisted Housekeeping and Maintenance

AI-powered housekeeping and maintenance tools can optimize staff productivity. By analysing room occupancy and guest departure times, AI can create efficient room cleaning schedules, reducing wait times for check-ins. Moreover, AI can assist in predictive maintenance, flagging potential issues with equipment before they escalate, allowing staff to address them proactively.

Personalizing Guest Recommendations

AI can collaborate with hotel staff to offer personalized recommendations for guests. By analysing guest data, AI can suggest tailored experiences, such as recommending spa treatments based on previous preferences or suggesting activities aligned with individual interests. Staff can then use these AI-driven insights to curate customized itineraries, elevating the guest experience and fostering guest loyalty.

Training and Upskilling Staff in AI

To fully harness the benefits of AI, hotel staff may require training and upskilling in AI-related tools and technologies. Training programs can help staff become proficient in using AI-driven systems and understanding how to leverage AI insights to enhance their services. Investing in staff training ensures that they are equipped to work collaboratively with AI and embrace the technological advancements that drive the hotel's success.

Conclusion

AI's collaboration with hotel staff enhances their capabilities and elevates guest experiences to new heights. By empowering staff with AI insights, streamlining customer support with chatbots, leveraging AI for housekeeping and maintenance, hotels can optimize their operations and deliver exceptional service. The combination of human expertise and AI-driven insights creates a powerful synergy that fosters guest satisfaction, loyalty, and a seamless guest journey. As business owners and managers in the hospitality industry, embracing AI as a collaborative tool empowers your staff to excel in their roles, strengthens guest relationships, and positions your hotel for continued success in an increasingly AI-driven world.

FUTURE TRENDS: AI INNOVATIONS RESHAPING THE HOSPITALITY LANDSCAPE

In this final chapter, we'll delve into the future trends of AI in the hospitality industry and explore the innovations that are set to reshape the landscape of hospitality in the coming years.

Voice-Activated Assistants

Voice-activated AI assistants will become more prevalent in hotel rooms, allowing guests to control various room features, request services, and access information through simple voice commands. This technology will further enhance the guest experience and create a more seamless and intuitive stay.

Personalized In-Room Experiences

AI will enable hotels to create hyper-personalized in-room experiences. Guest preferences, room settings, and entertainment options will be tailored based on individual preferences, making guests feel truly at home.

AI-Enhanced Loyalty Programs

AI will play a crucial role in loyalty programs, predicting guest preferences and offering targeted rewards and incentives. Hotels will use AI to design loyalty programs that are highly engaging and encourage repeat visits.

AI-Driven Revenue Management

AI-powered revenue management will continue to evolve, considering factors beyond traditional data. Hotels will integrate external data sources, such as social media trends and local events, to optimize pricing strategies and capture market opportunities.

Robotics in Hospitality

AI-powered robots will be increasingly integrated into hospitality operations. Robots can handle tasks such as delivering room service, assisting with luggage, and providing information to guests, enhancing efficiency and freeing up staff for more personalized services.

Contactless and Biometric Technology

Contactless solutions and biometric technology will become more sophisticated, enabling guests to have seamless and secure interactions with hotel services. From contactless check-in and check-out to facial recognition for access control, these technologies will shape the future of hospitality.

Virtual Reality (VR) and Augmented Reality (AR) Experiences

AI-powered VR and AR technologies will revolutionize how guests experience hotels before and during their stay. VR tours and AR navigation systems will allow guests to explore and interact with hotel amenities virtually, enhancing pre-booking experiences and making on-site navigation more engaging.

Sustainable AI Solutions

Hotels will increasingly adopt AI solutions that focus on sustainability. AI will be used to optimize energy consumption, reduce waste, and support eco-friendly practices, aligning with guests' growing demand for environmentally responsible hospitality.

Hyper-Personalized Marketing

AI will drive hyper-personalized marketing campaigns, enabling hotels to send highly targeted offers and promotions based on individual guest preferences and behaviours. This level of personalization will significantly impact guest engagement and conversion rates.

AI-Driven Health and Safety Measures

In the wake of the COVID-19 pandemic, AI will continue to play a role in ensuring health and safety in hotels. AI-powered thermal scanners, occupancy monitoring systems, and contactless technologies will be employed to provide a safe and secure environment for guests.

Conclusion

The future of the hospitality industry is intertwined with AI innovations that promise to reshape the guest experience and redefine hotel operations. As AI technologies continue to advance, hotels must embrace these trends to remain competitive and meet the evolving expectations of tech-savvy travellers. By adopting AI-driven solutions and striking the right balance between technology and human touch, hotels can create a harmonious blend of innovative experiences and genuine hospitality, securing their place at the forefront of the ever-evolving hospitality landscape.

SUCCESSFUL CASE STUDIES: REAL-WORLD APPLICATIONS OF AI IN HOTELS

In this chapter, we'll explore real-world case studies of hotels that have successfully implemented AI technologies to enhance guest experiences, streamline operations, and achieve remarkable results in the hospitality industry.

Case Study 1: AI-Driven Personalization at a Luxury Resort

A luxury resort in a popular tourist destination embraced AI-driven personalization to create unforgettable experiences for its guests. By leveraging AI analytics on guest data, the resort could predict guest preferences and behaviour accurately. The resort used this data to curate personalized itineraries, recommend bespoke experiences, and even customize room settings based on guest preferences. This level of personalization significantly increased guest satisfaction and loyalty. Additionally, the resort implemented AI chatbots for customer support, providing quick responses to guest inquiries and freeing up staff to focus on delivering personalized services.

Case Study 2: AI-Enhanced Revenue Management at a Business Hotel

A business hotel implemented AI-powered revenue management to optimize room rates based on demand fluctuations and market trends. The AI algorithms analysed data from various sources, including competitor rates, local events, and historical booking patterns. As a result, the hotel achieved higher room occupancy rates during peak periods and maximized revenue during low-demand periods. The ability to adjust pricing dynamically based on real-time data significantly improved the hotel's bottom line.

Case Study 3: AI-Powered Robotics at a Tech-Savvy Boutique Hotel

A tech-savvy boutique hotel integrated AI-powered robots into its operations to deliver a futuristic guest experience. Robots were deployed to handle room service deliveries, assist guests with luggage, and provide information about hotel amenities and nearby attractions. Guests were fascinated by the presence of robots, and the efficiency of robotic services garnered positive reviews. The hotel's innovative use of AI-powered robots set it apart from competitors and positioned it as a unique and memorable destination.

Case Study 4: AI-Driven Chatbots for Instant Guest Support at a Resort Chain

A resort chain with multiple properties worldwide implemented AI-driven chatbots to provide instant guest support across all locations. Guests could use chatbots to inquire about resort amenities, make reservations, and get recommendations for activities. The chatbots offered multilingual support, catering to the diverse international clientele. This streamlined customer support, reduced response times, and improved guest satisfaction across the entire resort chain.

Case Study 5: AI-Enabled Sustainability Initiatives at an Eco-Resort

An eco-resort integrated AI into its sustainability initiatives to optimize energy consumption and waste management. AI-powered energy management systems monitored energy usage throughout the property and adjusted heating, cooling, and lighting based on occupancy levels. Additionally, AI analytics were used to identify waste reduction opportunities and optimize recycling efforts. The resort's commitment to sustainable practices, driven by AI technologies, appealed to eco-conscious travellers, attracting a growing number of environmentally aware guests.

Conclusion

These real-world case studies demonstrate the tangible benefits of AI in the hospitality industry. From AI-driven personalization to revenue optimization, robotics, and sustainability initiatives, hotels across the globe are leveraging AI to enhance guest experiences and improve operational efficiency. As business owners and managers in the hospitality sector, understanding the success stories of AI implementation serves as inspiration and motivation to explore and embrace AI technologies in your own establishments. By taking cues from these case studies, hotels can embark on their own journey towards successful AI integration.

AI ADOPTION ROADMAP: STRATEGIES FOR EMBRACING AI IN YOUR HOTEL

In this chapter, we'll provide a step-by-step roadmap for hotels looking to embrace AI technologies and successfully integrate them into their operations.

Step 1: Assessing Your Needs and Objectives

Begin by conducting a comprehensive assessment of your hotel's needs and objectives. Identify areas where AI can make a significant impact, such as guest personalization, revenue management, operational efficiency, or sustainability initiatives. Determine clear goals for AI implementation that align with your overall business strategy.

Step 2: Building a Cross-Functional Team

Form a cross-functional team that includes representatives from various departments, such as operations, marketing, IT, and guest services. This team will collaborate on AI adoption, bringing diverse perspectives and expertise to the decision-making process.

Step 3: Evaluating AI Solutions and Vendors

Research and evaluate AI solutions and vendors that align with your hotel's needs and objectives. Look for reputable vendors with experience in the hospitality industry and a track record of successful AI implementations. Request demos and pilot projects to assess how well the AI solutions fit your hotel's requirements.

Step 4: Data Collection and Management

Ensure your hotel has a robust data collection and management system in place. Clean, accurate, and relevant data is essential for AI to provide valuable insights. Consider investing in data management tools and practices to centralize and organize data from various sources.

Step 5: Staff Training and Change Management

Prepare your staff for AI adoption through comprehensive training programs. Equip them with the knowledge and skills needed to collaborate effectively with AI technologies. Address any concerns or resistance to change through open communication and reassurance about AI's role in enhancing their work rather than replacing it.

Step 6: Pilot Projects and Testing

Start with pilot projects to test the effectiveness of AI solutions in specific areas. Pilot projects allow you to evaluate the feasibility and impact of AI in a controlled environment before implementing it on a broader scale.

Step 7: Implementing AI Solutions

Once pilot projects prove successful, proceed with the implementation of AI solutions across relevant areas of your hotel's operations. Gradually roll out AI technologies to different departments, allowing for adjustments and refinements based on real-world feedback.

Step 8: Monitoring and Optimization

Continuously monitor the performance of AI technologies and gather feedback from guests and staff. Use data-driven insights to optimize AI solutions, ensuring they align with evolving guest preferences and business goals.

Step 9: Guest Communication and Transparency

Communicate with guests about the AI technologies you have implemented and how they enhance their experiences. Emphasize the importance of guest privacy and transparent data usage. Engage guests in the AI-driven enhancements you've made to create a positive perception of technology adoption.

Step 10: Embracing a Culture of Innovation

Encourage a culture of innovation within your hotel, where the adoption of new technologies, including AI, is celebrated. Reward and recognize staff members who embrace AI and contribute to its successful integration.

Conclusion

Embracing AI in your hotel requires careful planning, collaboration, and a commitment to innovation. By following this roadmap, you can navigate the process of AI adoption, ensuring that AI technologies enrich guest experiences, drive operational efficiency, and position your hotel for success in the technologically advanced future of the hospitality industry.

THE VALUE PROPOSITION: WHY SMALL HOTEL OWNERS SHOULD INVEST IN AI

In this chapter, we'll explore the compelling value proposition of AI for small hotel owners, highlighting the tangible benefits that AI technologies can bring to their establishments. As the hospitality industry evolves with technological advancements, small hotels have a unique opportunity to leverage AI to their advantage. By adopting AI-driven solutions, small hotel owners can enhance guest experiences, optimize operations, and stay competitive in a rapidly changing landscape.

Enhanced Guest Experiences

In today's hospitality landscape, guest expectations are higher than ever before. Travelers seek personalized and memorable experiences that cater to their unique preferences and interests. AI-driven personalization enables small hotels to offer tailored experiences that resonate with individual guests. By analysing guest data, AI algorithms can understand guest preferences, stay histories, and spending behaviour, allowing hotels to anticipate guest needs and deliver a personalized touch throughout their stay.

Imagine a small boutique hotel that leverages AI to create hyper-personalized guest experiences. Upon check-in, the AI system greets guests by name and customizes room settings, such as temperature and lighting, based on their past preferences. The hotel's AI-powered recommendation system suggests nearby attractions, activities, and restaurants tailored to each guest's interests. As guests explore the city, the AI system sends timely promotions and offers for experiences they are likely to enjoy. This level of personalization leaves a lasting impression on guests, leading to higher satisfaction, positive reviews, and increased loyalty.

Operational Efficiency and Cost Savings

In addition to elevating guest experiences, AI can significantly enhance hotel operations and lead to cost savings. Managing various aspects of a hotel's operations can be complex, especially for small establishments with limited resources. AI technologies offer automation and optimization solutions that streamline processes, reduce manual workloads, and improve efficiency.

For instance, AI-driven revenue management systems can help small hotels optimize room rates based on demand fluctuations and market trends. These systems analyse data from various sources, including competitor rates, local events, and historical booking patterns, to determine the ideal pricing strategy. By dynamically adjusting room rates, small hotels can maximize revenue during peak periods and attract guests during low-demand periods. This data-driven approach to revenue management can significantly impact the hotel's bottom line, ensuring revenue optimization throughout the year.

Moreover, AI-powered systems can assist in inventory management, helping hotels optimize stock levels for consumables and amenities. By tracking inventory data and guest consumption patterns, AI can ensure that hotels maintain adequate supplies without overstocking, reducing waste and cutting operational costs.

Competitive Edge in the Market

In a highly competitive hospitality market, small hotels must differentiate themselves to attract and retain guests. AI technologies offer small hotels a competitive edge by enabling them to deliver cutting-edge services that appeal to modern travellers. For example, small hotels can integrate AI chatbots into their website and mobile apps to provide instant guest support. These chatbots can handle routine inquiries, provide information about hotel amenities, and assist with reservation requests, enhancing the overall customer experience. The availability of AI-powered chat support sets the hotel apart as tech-savvy and customer-focused, appealing to a tech-savvy clientele.

Furthermore, voice-activated assistants, powered by AI, are becoming increasingly popular in the hospitality industry. By incorporating voice assistants into guest rooms, small hotels can offer guests a seamless and convenient way to control room features, request services, and access information using simple voice commands. This cutting-edge feature creates a unique selling point for the hotel and attracts guests looking for a modern and innovative stay experience.

Revenue Optimization

A primary objective for any hotel is to maximize revenue while ensuring high guest satisfaction. AI-powered revenue management systems can play a pivotal role in achieving this goal. These systems analyse a vast amount of data, including historical booking patterns, competitor rates, local events, and guest preferences, to optimize room rates and yield management.

For small hotels, revenue optimization is crucial for maintaining financial stability and profitability. By leveraging AI to adjust room rates dynamically based on real-time data, small hotels can respond swiftly to changes in demand, ensuring that room rates align with market conditions. As a result, small hotels can optimize their pricing strategies, achieve higher occupancy rates during peak periods, and maximize revenue during low-demand periods.

By adopting AI-driven revenue management solutions, small hotels can compete more effectively with larger establishments and achieve higher financial returns, positioning them for sustainable growth in the long run.

Guest Loyalty and Repeat Business

Loyalty is a key driver of success in the hospitality industry. Satisfied and loyal guests are more likely to return to a hotel for future stays and recommend it to others, contributing to the hotel's reputation and word-of-mouth marketing.

AI-powered personalization plays a significant role in fostering guest loyalty. By using AI to analyse guest preferences and behaviour, small hotels can understand individual guest needs and deliver personalized services that exceed expectations.

Consider a small luxury hotel that leverages AI to enhance guest loyalty. The AI system tracks guest preferences, such as room settings, dining preferences, and preferred amenities. When a returning guest makes a reservation, the AI system recognizes them and ensures that their preferred settings are ready upon arrival. Additionally, the hotel's AI-powered loyalty program offers personalized rewards and incentives based on the guest's stay history and spending behaviour.

This level of personalization creates a sense of connection and appreciation, motivating guests to return to the hotel for future stays. The hotel's investment in AI-driven loyalty programs pays off through increased guest retention and positive word-of-mouth, contributing to a loyal customer base and sustained business growth.

Operational Insights and Data-Driven Decision Making

Data is a valuable asset in the hospitality industry, providing crucial insights that drive informed decision-making. AI technologies are adept at analysing vast amounts of data quickly and accurately, generating actionable insights that help hotel owners make informed choices.

For small hotel owners, data-driven decision-making can be a game-changer. AI analytics can provide operational insights into areas such as guest preferences, revenue trends, demand patterns, and staff performance. With access to these insights, small hotel owners can identify opportunities for improvement, implement targeted marketing strategies, and allocate resources effectively.

Imagine a small boutique hotel that uses AI analytics to understand guest preferences. The AI system analyses guest data to identify popular amenities, services, and activities among different guest segments. Armed with this information, the hotel can create targeted marketing campaigns to attract specific guest demographics and promote relevant experiences.

Additionally, AI can optimize staff scheduling based on demand forecasts, ensuring that the hotel has the right number of staff members to deliver exceptional service during peak periods while avoiding overstaffing during low-demand periods.

By embracing data-driven decision-making through AI technologies, small hotel owners can optimize their operations, enhance service quality, and stay agile in a dynamic market.

Time-Saving Automation

The hospitality industry involves numerous routine tasks that can consume valuable staff time. AI-driven automation can streamline these tasks, allowing staff to focus on delivering personalized and attentive service to guests.

For example, AI-powered chatbots can handle routine guest inquiries and reservation confirmations, freeing up front desk staff to engage in more meaningful interactions with guests. Chatbots can provide instant responses to frequently asked questions, such as check-in and check-out times, nearby attractions, and hotel amenities. Moreover, chatbots can operate 24/7, providing round-the-clock support to guests regardless of staff availability.

AI automation can also extend to back-office functions. For instance, AI can assist in inventory management, automatically ordering supplies when stock levels are low, and tracking consumption patterns to avoid waste. This automation not only saves staff time but also reduces the likelihood of human errors in inventory management.

By leveraging AI automation, small hotels can optimize staff resources, increase productivity, and allocate more time to delivering exceptional guest experiences.

Sustainable Practices and Environmental Responsibility

As travellers become more environmentally conscious, sustainable practices are gaining importance in the hospitality industry. AI can play a pivotal role in supporting small hotels' efforts to implement eco-friendly initiatives and reduce their environmental footprint.

AI-powered energy management systems can optimize energy consumption by adjusting heating, cooling, and lighting based on guest occupancy patterns and preferences. By monitoring and analysing energy usage data, hotels can identify opportunities to reduce energy waste and enhance energy efficiency.

For example, a small eco-resort might integrate AI analytics into its sustainability initiatives. The AI system tracks energy usage patterns in guest rooms and common areas, identifying areas where energy consumption can be reduced without compromising guest comfort. The resort's commitment to sustainable practices resonates with environmentally conscious travellers and contributes to the hotel's reputation as an eco-friendly destination.

Additionally, AI can support waste reduction efforts by optimizing inventory management and minimizing overstocking. By tracking consumption patterns and adjusting inventory levels accordingly, hotels can reduce waste and contribute to sustainable operations.

Flexibility and Scalability

One of the advantages of AI technologies is their flexibility and scalability. AI solutions can be tailored to meet the specific needs and budget constraints of small hotels. Whether a hotel has a few rooms or a larger property, AI technologies can be implemented and customized to suit the establishment's size and requirements.

Furthermore, AI technologies are designed to be adaptable to changing business needs and market conditions. As the hotel grows or the industry evolves, AI systems can be updated and expanded to accommodate new challenges and opportunities.

For small hotel owners, this flexibility allows them to start small with AI adoption, gradually integrating AI solutions into different aspects of their operations. As they witness the benefits and the positive impact on guest experiences and business performance, they can scale up their AI investments strategically.

Future-Proofing Your Business

In a rapidly changing technological landscape, future-proofing your business is essential for long-term success. AI technologies are at the forefront of hospitality innovations, and their influence on the industry is only expected to grow.

Investing in AI technologies positions small hotels for sustainable growth and competitiveness in the future. By embracing AI early on, small hotel owners can capitalize on emerging trends and stay ahead of competitors.

As technology continues to advance, AI will play an increasingly critical role in the hospitality industry. Small hotels that integrate AI into their operations today will be better prepared to navigate future challenges and take advantage of new opportunities.

Conclusion

AI technologies offer a compelling value proposition for small hotel owners looking to enhance guest experiences, optimize operations, and stay competitive in a fast-paced hospitality industry. By adopting AI-driven solutions, small hotels can deliver personalized services that resonate with guests, optimize revenue and operational efficiency, and position themselves for sustained growth.

Enhanced guest experiences through AI-driven personalization create a lasting impression on guests, driving loyalty and repeat business. AI-powered revenue optimization ensures that small hotels maximize their revenue potential, even during periods of fluctuating demand. Data-driven decision-making through AI analytics empowers small hotel owners to make informed choices that drive positive outcomes.

AI automation streamlines routine tasks, saving staff time and increasing operational efficiency. Sustainability initiatives supported by AI technologies align with the preferences of eco-conscious travellers, contributing to the hotel's reputation as an environmentally responsible destination.

Furthermore, AI solutions are flexible and scalable, catering to the unique needs and budget constraints of small hotels. By future-proofing their business with AI adoption, small hotel owners position themselves for continued success in an ever-evolving industry.

As small hotel owners explore the possibilities of AI technologies, it is essential to approach AI adoption strategically. Building a cross-functional team, evaluating AI solutions and vendors, and starting with pilot projects are essential steps to ensure a smooth and successful integration of AI into the hotel's operations.

With a clear focus on guest satisfaction, operational efficiency, and future readiness, small hotel owners can unlock the full potential of AI technologies, creating a positive impact on their guests, staff, and overall business performance.

PRACTICAL AI INTEGRATION: IMPLEMENTING AI IN EXISTING HOTELS WITHOUT INFRASTRUCTURE OVERHAUL

In this chapter, we'll explore practical strategies for integrating AI technologies into existing hotels without the need for a complete infrastructure overhaul. For many small and medium-sized hotels, the idea of adopting AI might seem daunting, especially if they have existing systems in place. However, with careful planning and step-by-step implementation, hotels can successfully integrate AI into their operations and reap the benefits of enhanced guest experiences, improved efficiency, and increased competitiveness.

Conducting a Technology Audit

Before embarking on AI integration, it's essential to conduct a comprehensive technology audit of the hotel's current systems and processes. Identify areas that can benefit from AI solutions and assess the compatibility of existing systems with potential AI technologies. This audit will provide a clear picture of where AI can add value and how it can align with the hotel's existing technology infrastructure.

Identifying Priority Areas for AI Adoption

AI offers a wide range of applications in the hospitality industry, but implementing AI across all areas simultaneously may not be feasible or cost-effective for existing hotels. Identify priority areas where AI can have the most significant impact on guest experiences and operational efficiency.

Common priority areas for AI integration include:

- Guest personalization and recommendation systems
- Revenue management and dynamic pricing
- Customer support and chatbots
- Energy management and sustainability initiatives
- Predictive maintenance for facilities and equipment
- Data analytics for business insights

Focus on one or two priority areas initially, and gradually expand AI adoption to other areas over time.

Collaboration with Existing Technology Providers

Many hotels have existing technology partners and vendors providing services such as property management systems (PMS), customer relationship management (CRM) platforms, and booking engines. When considering AI integration, collaborate with these existing technology providers to explore AI solutions that can seamlessly integrate with the hotel's current systems.

Working with familiar technology partners can simplify the integration process and ensure that AI solutions complement the hotel's existing infrastructure. Vendors may offer AI add-ons or upgrades to their existing products, facilitating a smoother transition.

Selecting AI Solutions that Fit Your Needs

When choosing AI solutions, consider factors such as the hotel's size, budget, and specific requirements. Look for AI technologies that offer scalability and flexibility, allowing the hotel to start with a smaller implementation and gradually expand as needed.

Cloud-based AI platforms can be particularly advantageous for existing hotels, as they eliminate the need for extensive hardware upgrades and provide greater accessibility and adaptability. Cloud-based solutions also offer regular updates and maintenance, ensuring that the hotel benefits from the latest AI advancements.

Pilot Projects for Testing and Learning

Before implementing AI solutions across the entire hotel, conduct pilot projects in the identified priority areas. Pilot projects involve implementing AI technologies on a small scale to test their effectiveness and gather feedback from staff and guests.

For instance, a pilot project might involve deploying an AI-powered chatbot for customer support on the hotel's website. The chatbot can handle guest inquiries, provide information about room availability, and answer frequently asked questions. During the pilot phase, monitor the chatbot's performance and collect feedback from guests to identify areas for improvement.

Pilot projects not only allow hotels to validate the effectiveness of AI technologies but also provide valuable insights into the hotel's readiness for AI adoption.

Staff Training and Change Management

The successful integration of AI in existing hotels relies on staff readiness and acceptance. Implement comprehensive staff training programs to familiarize employees with AI technologies and their role in enhancing guest experiences and operational efficiency.

Train staff on how to use AI systems effectively, interpret AI-generated insights, and leverage AI capabilities to deliver personalized guest services. Emphasize the complementary nature of AI, highlighting how it enhances human capabilities rather than replacing them.

Open communication and transparent change management are essential to addressing any concerns or resistance among staff members. Addressing staff queries and providing reassurance about the positive impact of AI can foster a culture of acceptance and enthusiasm for AI integration.

Data Management and Privacy

AI technologies rely on data to generate insights and make personalized recommendations. Ensure that the hotel has robust data management practices in place to collect, store, and protect guest data securely.

Implement data privacy measures to comply with relevant regulations and ensure that guest data is used responsibly and transparently. Assure guests that their data is safe and that AI technologies are used to enhance their experiences and not compromise their privacy.

Integrating AI with Human Touch

One of the key considerations in AI integration is striking the right balance between technology and the human touch. AI should enhance, not replace, the personal connections between staff and guests.

Encourage staff to use AI-generated insights to offer personalized services and create memorable experiences for guests. Emphasize the importance of human empathy, intuition, and interpersonal skills in delivering exceptional hospitality.

Continuous Evaluation and Improvement

AI integration is an ongoing process that requires continuous evaluation and improvement. Regularly assess the impact of AI technologies on guest experiences, staff productivity, and operational efficiency. Gather feedback from guests and staff to identify areas for optimization and refinement.

Stay updated on the latest AI advancements and emerging trends in the hospitality industry. AI technologies are constantly evolving, and staying informed about new innovations can help hotels stay ahead of the competition and continue to deliver cutting-edge services.

Celebrating Success and Sharing Best Practices

As AI integration progresses, celebrate successes and share best practices with staff and industry peers. Recognize staff members who excel in leveraging AI technologies to deliver outstanding guest experiences. Sharing success stories can motivate staff and create a positive culture of innovation within the hotel.

Furthermore, participate in industry forums and conferences to learn from other hotels' AI experiences and share your own insights. Collaboration with peers and learning from their AI journeys can provide valuable knowledge and inspiration for continuous improvement.

Conclusion

AI integration in existing hotels is a strategic process that requires careful planning, collaboration, and an open mindset towards technological innovation. By conducting a technology audit, identifying priority areas, collaborating with existing technology providers, selecting AI solutions that fit the hotel's needs, existing hotels can successfully integrate AI without the need for a complete infrastructure overhaul.

Pilot projects allow hotels to test AI technologies, gather feedback, make informed decisions about expanding AI adoption. Staff training and change management are crucial to ensure that employees embrace AI as a complementary tool that enhances their capabilities.

Data management and privacy measures ensure that AI technologies leverage guest data responsibly and transparently, building trust with guests. Integrating AI with human touch ensures that technology enhances rather than replaces personal connections between staff members.

Continuous evaluation and improvement are essential for ongoing AI success, as hotels strive to deliver cutting-edge experiences and stay ahead of industry trends. Celebrating success and sharing best practices foster a culture of innovation and inspire hotels to push the boundaries of AI integration.

By following practical strategies for AI integration, existing hotels can unlock the full potential of AI technologies, enhancing guest experiences, improving operational efficiency, and positioning themselves for success in an ever-evolving hospitality landscape.

FINAL THOUGHTS: THE ROAD AHEAD - EMBRACING A TECHNOLOGICAL FUTURE IN HOSPITALITY

As we conclude this exploration of the rise of AI in the hospitality industry and its potential paradigm shift in the hotel sector, it becomes evident that the future of hospitality lies in embracing technological advancements. AI has the potential to revolutionize the way hotels operate, interact with guests, and deliver exceptional experiences.

The Promise of AI in Hospitality

AI technologies offer unparalleled opportunities for hotels to enhance guest experiences, optimize operations, and stay competitive in a rapidly changing landscape. From personalized guest interactions to AI-driven revenue management and sustainability initiatives, the benefits of AI are compelling and transformative.

By embracing AI, hotels can elevate their service standards, anticipate guest needs, and create memorable experiences that foster guest loyalty and advocacy. AI-powered automation streamlines routine tasks, freeing up staff to focus on meaningful interactions with guests and deliver genuine hospitality.

Navigating Challenges

While the promise of AI in hospitality is vast, embracing this technological future comes with challenges. One of the primary concerns is ensuring a seamless integration of AI with the human touch. While AI can enhance guest interactions, it should complement, not replace, the warmth and empathy that only human staff can provide.

Data privacy and security are also critical considerations when leveraging AI in guest engagement and data analytics. Hotels must prioritize the responsible use of guest data, ensuring transparency and obtaining guest consent for data collection and utilization.

Moreover, AI adoption requires adequate staff training and change management to ensure that employees are empowered to leverage AI technologies effectively. Hotels must foster a culture of continuous learning and innovation, encouraging staff to embrace AI as a tool that enhances their capabilities and improves guest experiences.

Strategies for Success

To fully harness the potential of AI in hospitality, hotels must approach AI adoption strategically. Conducting technology audits, identifying priority areas for AI integration, and collaborating with existing technology providers are essential steps to create a solid foundation for AI implementation.

Pilot projects enable hotels to test AI technologies on a small scale, gather feedback, and refine their approach before scaling up. Hotels must also invest in staff training to ensure that employees are proficient in using AI tools and understand their role in delivering personalized guest experiences.

Embracing a Culture of Innovation

Embracing a technological future in hospitality requires a culture of innovation and openness to change. Hotels must be willing to explore emerging AI trends, collaborate with industry peers, and share best practices to stay at the forefront of AI integration.

By fostering a culture of innovation, hotels can create a competitive advantage and position themselves as pioneers in leveraging AI to redefine guest experiences and operational excellence.

Collaboration and Partnership

The road ahead for AI integration in hospitality is not solitary. Collaboration and partnership with AI vendors, technology providers, and industry experts play a crucial role in navigating the complexities of AI adoption.

By collaborating with trusted partners, hotels can access specialized expertise, AI solutions tailored to their needs, and ongoing support to ensure a successful AI implementation.

Embracing Sustainability

As hotels integrate AI technologies, they must also be mindful of their environmental impact. AI can support sustainability initiatives by optimizing energy consumption, reducing waste, and supporting eco-friendly practices.

Hotels must embrace sustainability as a core value, leveraging AI to make environmentally responsible decisions and reduce their carbon footprint. Sustainability initiatives are not only ethically sound but also resonate with environmentally conscious travellers.

Looking Ahead: An Exciting Future

The future of hospitality with AI is bright and promising. As AI technologies continue to evolve, hotels will have access to even more innovative solutions that further enhance guest experiences and operational efficiency.

From advancements in emotional AI and natural language processing to AI-powered robotics and virtual reality, the possibilities are boundless. Hotels that embrace AI early and stay agile in their approach will be best positioned to leverage these technological advancements for continued growth and success.

Embracing the Journey

As we navigate the path to a technological future in hospitality, it is essential to view AI not as a replacement for human touch but as an enabler of exceptional guest experiences. AI technologies can complement human capabilities, empowering hotel staff to deliver personalized and authentic hospitality.

As hotel owners, managers, and industry leaders, embracing AI is not just about keeping up with trends; it's about embracing a philosophy of innovation and continuous improvement. By embracing AI-driven guest engagement, optimizing operations, and fostering a culture of collaboration and sustainability, hotels can forge a unique and prosperous path into the future of hospitality.

Together, we embark on an exciting journey to reshape the hospitality landscape through AI innovation. As we move forward, let us remember that at the heart of every technological advancement is the genuine desire to create memorable experiences for our guests, making their journeys truly exceptional and unforgettable.

Embracing a Technological Future in Hospitality - The Journey Continues...

www.ingramcontent.com/pod-product-compliance
Lightning Source LLC
Chambersburg PA
CBHW072343290526
45794CB00002B/990